Mathalon Maps

Number Crunch Your Way Around the World

NORTH AMERICA

Joanne Randolph

raintree

a Capstone company — publishers for children

Raintree is an imprint of Capstone Global Library Limited, a company incorporated in England and Wales having its registered office at 264 Banbury Road, Oxford OX2 7DY – Registered company number: 6695582

www.raintree.co.uk
myorders@raintree.co.uk

Produced for Raintree by Calcium
Edited by Sarah Eason and Katie Woolley
Designed by Paul Myerscough
Illustrations by Moloko88/Shutterstock
Picture research by Sarah Eason
Production by Victoria Fitzgerald
Originated by Capstone Global Library Ltd © 2016
Printed and bound in China

ISBN 978 1 4747 1596 6
19 18 17 16 15
10 9 8 7 6 5 4 3 2 1

British Library Cataloguing in Publication Data
A full catalogue record for this book is available from the British Library.

Acknowledgements
We would like to thank the following for permission to reproduce photographs: Dreamstime: Dan Breckwoldt 28l; Shutterstock: American Spirit 11t, Thorsteinn Asgeirsson 5t, Rudy Balasko 11br, Gerardo Borbolla 4b, Darren J. Bradley 21b, Dan Breckwoldt 7br, Jo Crebbin 8l, Critterbiz 22bl, Songquan Deng 5b, 29b, Anton Foltin 20r, 27c, Arto Hakola 20l, Holbox 26l, Jerry Horbert 13c, JoMo333 8br, Kan Khampanya 23t, Jessica Kirsh 16c, Patryk Kosmider 18l, Jess Kraft 18r, LehaKoK 22-23b, Lemon Seven 16b, David Malik 10, MarkVanDykePhotography 9b, V. J. Matthew 9t, Michal K. 25t, Outdoorsman 6c, 29t, Sean Pavone 13t, Mike Peters 24, Piotreknik 19b, Aleksei Potov 6t, Rigucci 17br, Iriana Shiyan 5c, Siouxsnapp 13b, B. G. Smith 25br, Worachat Sodsri 27t, Somchaij 1, 15t, SurangaSL 27b, Tusharkoley 14r.

Cover photographs reproduced with permission of: Dreamstime: Dan Breckwoldt (top); Shutterstock: Dennis W. Donohue (bottom), Jessica Kirsh (back cover).

Some words are shown in bold, **like this**. You can find out what they mean by looking in the glossary.

Contents

North America

North America is the third-largest **continent** on Earth. It has an area of about 24.6 million sq km (9.5 million sq miles). It has many different **geological** features, **ecosystems** and plants and animals that make it a one-of-a-kind place. Get ready to explore ... with maths!

How to use this book

Look for the "Map-a-stat" and "Do the maths" features and complete the maths challenges. Then look at the answers on pages 28 and 29 to see if your calculations are correct.

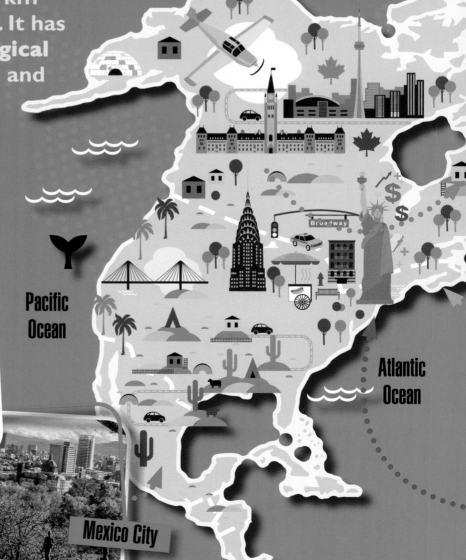

Arctic Ocean

Pacific Ocean

Atlantic Ocean

Mexico City

More than meets the eye

You may think of North America as being made up of Canada, the United States and Mexico. These are the largest countries that share the continent but there are 27 countries and territories in all. The countries in Central America, as well as many islands in the Caribbean Sea, are all part of the North American continent. **Greenland** is part of the North American continent, too, because it shares the same **tectonic plate**.

Map-a-stat

The United States is 4,312 km (2,680 miles) wide, from the East Coast to the West Coast.

The North American continent has a population of around 530 million.

The population of the United States is around 318 million.

Mexico has more than 120 million people, and Canada has around 35 million people.

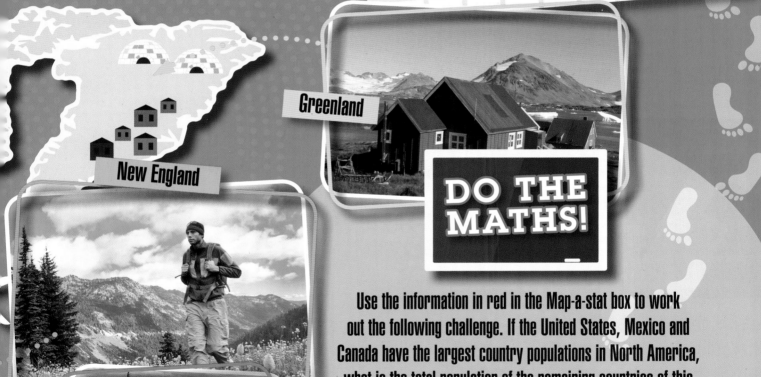

Greenland

New England

New York City

DO THE MATHS!

Use the information in red in the Map-a-stat box to work out the following challenge. If the United States, Mexico and Canada have the largest country populations in North America, what is the total population of the remaining countries of this continent? Here is the equation to help you solve the problem.

530,000,000 people − (318,000,000 + 120,000,000 + 35,000,000) = ? people

Complete the maths challenge, then turn to pages 28—29 to see if your calculation is correct!

O, Canada!

Canada is North America's largest country by area. Canada is also the second-largest country in the world. It has 10 provinces and three territories. While Canada has its own government and **constitution**, it recognizes the Queen of England as its **monarch**.

North versus South

Canada's capital is Ottawa, which is in Southern Ontario. Although Canada is larger than the United States, it has far fewer people. Around 75 per cent of the Canadian people live in the southern part of the country, close to the border with the United States. This is because the northern parts of the country can be freezing cold and the land there is not **fertile**.

Lake Moraine is in Alberta, Canada.

Yukon Territory

Northwest Territory

Nunavut Territory

Newfoundland and Labrador

Quebec

Alberta

Manitoba

Prince Edward Island

British Columbia

Ontario

New Brunswick

territory

province

Saskatchewan

Nova Scotia

Map-a-stat

At 8,890 km (5,525 miles) long, the border between the United States and Canada is the longest border between two countries.

Canada has the longest coastline in the world. It measures 202,080 km (125,556 miles).

Canada has 563 lakes that are larger than 100 sq km (39 sq miles).

There are up to 25,000 polar bears in the world. Of that number, 15,000 live in Canada.

polar bears

DO THE MATHS!

Use the information in red in the Map-a-stat box to work out the following challenge. How many polar bears live in places other than Canada? Here is the equation to help you solve the problem.

25,000 polar bears – 15,000 polar bears = ? polar bears

Complete the maths challenge, then turn to pages 28–29 to see if your calculation is correct!

The city of Vancouver is on the West Coast of Canada, in British Columbia.

East Coast

Newfoundland and Labrador in Canada sit along the East coast of North America. New Brunswick, Nova Scotia, Prince Edward Island and Quebec are along the East Coast, too. In the United States, the coast stretches from Maine to Florida. Maine and its Canadian neighbours have rocky shores and long, cold winters. As one heads south, the coasts become sandier and warmer. Beaches along North Carolina's Outer Banks and Florida are popular tourist stops, as are the islands in the Caribbean Sea.

Florida's Everglades

Florida is known for more than its beaches. It is also known for the Everglades, a giant **wetland** area that is home to hundreds of plant and animal **species**, including the American alligator. The Everglades are around 97 km (60 miles) wide and 160 km (100 miles) long.

A roseate spoonbill makes its home in Florida's Everglades.

Cape Charles, Virginia, sits on the Chesapeake Bay.

Map-a-stat

The Appalachian Mountains stretch 2,414 km (1,500 miles) from Newfoundland all the way to Alabama.

The highest peak in the eastern United States is Mount Mitchell in North Carolina, which is 2,037 m (6,684 ft.) tall.

The Outer Banks of North Carolina are a 320-km- (200 miles) long string of barrier islands and peninsulas.

In 1903, Wilbur and Orville Wright took advantage of the windy conditions on the Outer Banks to work on building and flying the first successful aeroplanes.

The highest point in Florida is only 105 m (345 ft.) above sea level. The average elevation of Florida is less than 15 m (50 ft.) above sea level.

Prince Edward Island

Appalachian Mountains

DO THE MATHS!

Use the information in red in the Map-a-stat box to work out the following challenge. Compare the highest peak on the East Coast with the highest point in Florida. How much taller is Mount Mitchell? Here is the equation to help you solve the problem.

2,037 m – 105 m = ? m taller

Complete the maths challenge, then turn to pages 28–29 to see if your calculation is correct!

The Midwestern United States

The Midwestern United States is made up of 12 states. These are Illinois, Indiana, Iowa, Kansas, Michigan, Minnesota, Missouri, Nebraska, North Dakota, Ohio, South Dakota and Wisconsin. Six of the Midwestern States border the Great Lakes. The region has many large cities, such as Chicago and St. Louis, but is also known for its many farms.

The Great Lakes

One of the defining geographic features of the Midwest is the Great Lakes. The five Great Lakes are Lake Superior, Lake Michigan, Lake Huron, Lake Erie and Lake Ontario. The Great Lakes are the largest freshwater system in the world. They cover 244,106 sq km (94,250 sq miles). Lake Superior is the largest lake in the world, measuring 82,103 sq km (31,700 sq miles).

South Haven Lighthouse is an historic feature on Lake Michigan.

Map-a-stat

The Gateway Arch in St. Louis, Missouri, is the tallest man-made monument in the United States. The top of the arch stands 192 m (630 ft.) tall.

Four out of five Great Lakes are part of the Midwest. The largest one is Lake Superior, which has a shore length of 2,782 km (1,729 miles).

The Mississippi River starts in the Midwest. It is 3,765 km (2,340 miles) long, and is an important waterway for transporting goods.

Chicago, Illinois, has more people than any other city in the Midwest.

DO THE MATHS!

Use the information in red in the Map-a-stat box to work out the following challenge. If you paddled around the shoreline of Lake Superior at a rate of 3.2 km per hour, how long would it take you to get back to where you started? Round up your answer. Here is the equation to help you solve the problem.

$$2{,}782 \text{ km} \div 3.2 \text{ km per hour} = ? \text{ hours}$$

Complete the maths challenge, then turn to pages 28–29 to see if your calculation is correct!

Gateway Arch, St. Louis

The Southern United States

The Southern United States is a region considered to consist of 12 states: **North Carolina**, **South Carolina**, **Georgia**, **Florida**, **Tennessee**, **Kentucky**, **Mississippi**, **Alabama**, **Arkansas**, **Louisiana**, **Oklahoma** and **Texas**.

The South borders the **Atlantic Ocean** to the east and the **Gulf of Mexico** to the south. The **plains** and **prairies** of Texas and Oklahoma form the western border of the South. There are many lakes, rivers, coasts, caves and mountains in the South.

Swamps, rivers and mountains

The South is home to some of the world's most important wetlands, rivers, swamplands and **bayous**. The Mississippi River ends in the South, flowing into the Gulf of Mexico at the port of New Orleans.

The South has some spectacular mountains. The Blue Ridge Mountains are part of the Appalachian Range and extend into North Carolina. They are known for their beautiful blue colour when seen from a distance. The Great Smoky Mountains are also part of the Appalachian Range and are found in Tennessee and North Carolina.

These are cotton fields in the Southern United States.

Kentucky
Tennessee
North Carolina
South Carolina
Oklahoma
Arkansas
Mississippi
Georgia
Alabama
Texas
Louisiana
Florida

Map-a-stat

After Alaska, Texas is the second-largest state. The state is 420,412 sq km (261,232 sq miles) in area.

Mammoth Cave in Kentucky is the longest-known cave system in the world. There are 644 km (400 miles) of mapped passageways in the cave.

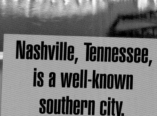

Nashville, Tennessee, is a well-known southern city.

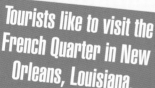

Tourists like to visit the French Quarter in New Orleans, Louisiana.

DO THE MATHS!

Use the information in red in the Map-a-stat box to work out the following challenge. If you were to walk at a speed of 3.2 km per hour, how many hours would it take you to walk the length of the Mammoth Cave and back again? Here is the equation to help you solve the problem.

$$(644 \text{ km} \div 3.2 \text{ km per hour}) \times 2 = ? \text{ hours}$$

Complete the maths challenge, then turn to pages 28—29 to see if your calculation is correct!

The Southwestern United States

The Southwest United States is considered to consist of five states: Arizona, New Mexico, Colorado, Utah and Nevada. The place where Colorado, Utah, Arizona and New Mexico meet is called the Four Corners. Sometimes, California, Texas and Oklahoma are included in the Southwest but only parts of these states are in the geographic Southwest.

Hot and dry

The Southwest has an **arid climate**. This means that there is little rainfall or vegetation. The Southwest has rivers, mountains, deserts, **mesas** and some prairies. There are also canyons in the region, such as the Grand Canyon. The Southwest is famous for some of its beautiful rock formations, such as the arches at Arches National Park in Utah. Carlsbad Caverns is a system of more than 300 underground caves in New Mexico.

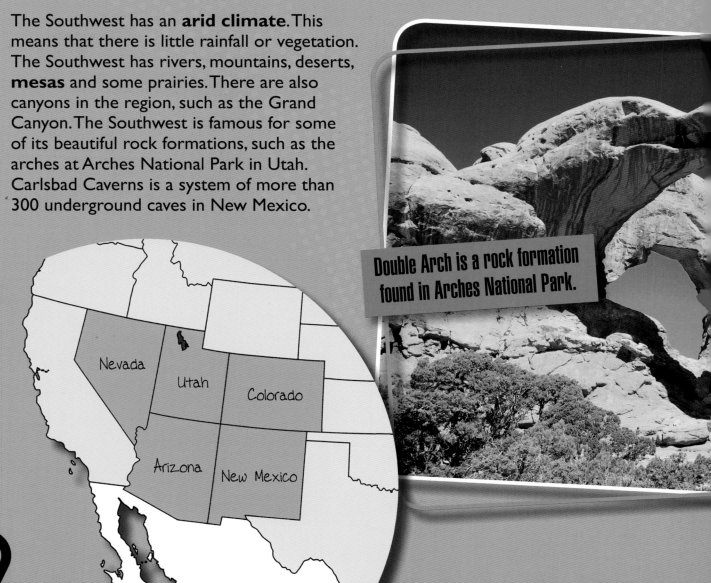

Double Arch is a rock formation found in Arches National Park.

Nevada

Utah

Colorado

Arizona

New Mexico

Map-a-stat

Carlsbad Caverns is the remains of a reef that was part of an inland sea, more than 250 million years ago.

Prairie dogs, which live in the Southwestern United States, among other places, are known for digging burrows up to 33 m (108 ft.) long.

Chaco Canyon in New Mexico has the ruins of a huge settlement built by native people more than 1,000 years ago. One of the structures there is thought to have been built from 5,000 trees and 50 million stone blocks!

Arches National Park in Utah has more than 2,000 natural stone arches. In order to be considered an arch, an opening between the stones must be at least 1 m (3 ft.) wide. Some arches are more than 91 m (300 ft.) across.

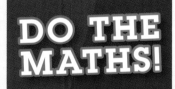

Use the information in red in the Map-a-stat box to work out the following challenge. What is the difference in width between the largest arches and the smallest? Here is the equation to help you solve the problem.

$$91 \, m - 1 \, m = ? \, m$$

Complete the maths challenge, then turn to pages 28—29 to see if your calculation is correct!

West Coast

The West Coast of the United States is made up of California, Oregon and Washington. Its eastern border is formed by the Sierra Nevada mountain range, the Cascade Range and the Mojave Desert. The West Coast also has some fertile regions, including the Puget Sound area in Washington, the Willamette Valley in Oregon and the Central Valley in California.

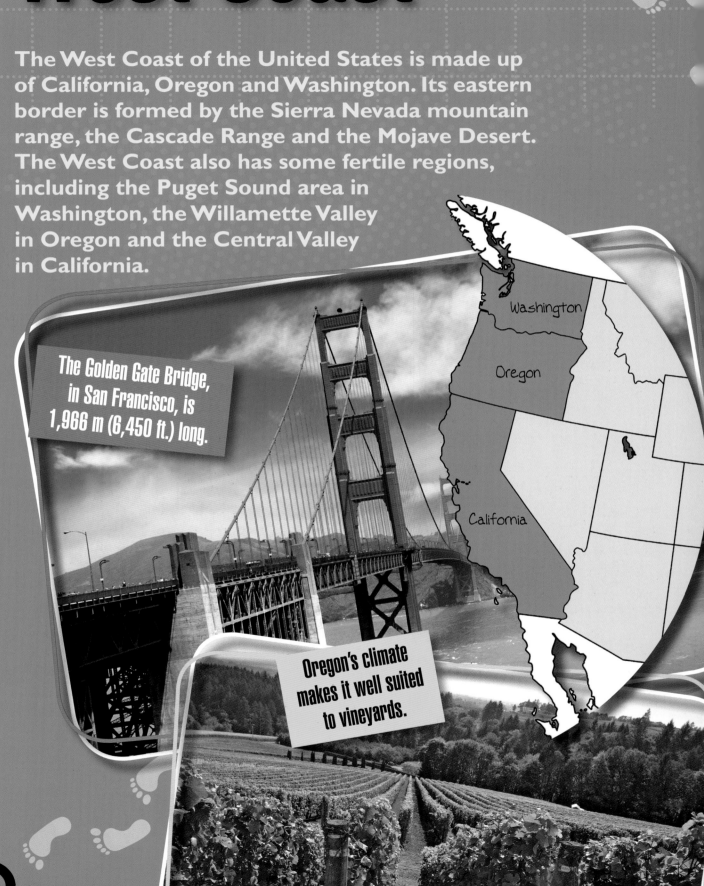

The Golden Gate Bridge, in San Francisco, is 1,966 m (6,450 ft.) long.

Washington

Oregon

California

Oregon's climate makes it well suited to vineyards.

Wilderness and cities

The Sierra Nevada, which is 400 km (250 miles) long and about 112 km (70 miles) wide, forms part of the eastern border of California. This range has many famous national forests and wilderness areas, such as Yosemite, Sequoia National Park and Lake Tahoe. The West Coast has many large cities, too. These include San Francisco, San Diego and Los Angeles in California; Portland in Oregon; and Seattle in Washington.

Map-a-stat

Death Valley, in California, is the hottest and lowest place in North America. It is 86 m (282 ft.) below sea level. The Dead Sea, between Israel and Jordan, is the lowest place on Earth at 418 m (1,371 ft.) below sea level.

The driving distance from San Diego to Los Angeles is 201 km (125 miles). It is another 613 km (381 miles) to drive from Los Angeles to San Francisco.

The West Coast has 33 national forests and huge areas of protected wilderness.

Seattle's Space Needle has a rotating restaurant and an observation deck from which to take in the city views. Including its antenna, the building is 184 m (605 ft.) tall.

DO THE MATHS!

Use the information in red in the Map-a-stat box to work out the following challenge. If you wanted to drive from San Diego to San Francisco with a stop in Los Angeles, how many km would you need to drive? Here is the equation to help you solve the problem.

$$201 \text{ km} + 613 \text{ km} = ? \text{ km}$$

Complete the maths challenge, then turn to pages 28—29 to see if your calculation is correct!

Space Needle, Seattle

Mexico

Mexico covers nearly 1,968,400 sq km (760,000 sq miles). It is made up of 31 states and a capital district. More than 120 million people make their home in Mexico. Some 200,000 species of plants and animals make their home there, too. Mexico has mountain ranges, many rivers and around 240,000 sq km (92,655 sq miles) of protected natural areas.

Mexico

The Caribbean Sea off Mexico's coast is home to many kinds of turtles.

Mexico City is Mexico's capital.

Rich in history

Mexico has 32 **World Heritage Sites**, including the Mayan ruins at Chichen Itza. Many of these historic sites are ruins from the ancient people who ruled in Mexico long ago, such as the Olmec, Toltec, Maya and Aztecs. Other sites remember the influence of the Spanish who came and **conquered** the ancient empires. Some of these sites simply **preserve** some of Mexico's natural beauty, such as the Gulf of California and the whale **sanctuary** off El Vizcaino.

Kukulkan Pyramid, Chichen Itza

Map-a-stat

Chichen Itza is a city that was built by the Mayan civilization around 1,000 years ago. El Castillo is the central temple of the city. Each side of the pyramid has a staircase with 91 steps. The pyramid is 24 m (78 ft.) tall.

Mexico is one of around 17 countries that are considered to be megadiverse. This means they are home to many different kinds of plants and animals. Mexico has around 200,000 known species. It has the second-highest number of reptiles in the world, with 804 species, and the third-highest number of mammals, with 535 species. It has 361 known amphibian species. It also has more than 23,424 different kinds of non-vascular plants!

The Large Millimeter Telescope in Mexico is the largest of its kind and was built to see areas in space that have a lot of dust. It has a diameter of 50 m (164 ft.).

DO THE MATHS!

Use the information in red in the Map-a-stat box to work out the following challenge. If you were to climb El Castillo at a rate of 1 step per second, how many minutes would it take you to reach the top of the temple? Round up your answer. Use this equation to help you solve the problem.

(91 steps ÷ 1 step per second) ÷ 60 seconds = ? minutes

Complete the maths challenge, then turn to pages 28—29 to see if your calculation is correct!

Deserts

Mojave Desert

Sonoran Desert

Great Basin Desert

Chihuahuan Desert

North America has four main deserts. These are the Chihuahuan Desert, the Great Basin Desert, the Mojave Desert and the Sonoran Desert. Most of these deserts are hot deserts, like the ones most of us think of when we imagine a desert. The Great Basin is considered a cold desert, though, because of its cooler temperatures and the kinds of plants and animals that live there.

Saguaro cactuses are found only in the Sonoran Desert.

This is a Great Basin collared lizard.

Desert animals

Deserts are difficult places in which to live, but many animals and plants find them the perfect spot to call home. Desert animals have **adapted** to life in these dry places. Jackrabbits have giant ears that help them stay cool. Desert tortoises spend their days inside burrows underground and only come out during the cooler nights. Some animals get all the water they need from the plants they eat, such as **cactuses**.

Map-a-stat

The Chihuahuan Desert covers more than 453,250 sq km (175,000 sq miles) of the United States and Mexico. Most of the desert gets less than 25 cm (10 in) of rain each year.

The Great Basin is the largest desert in the United States. It sits between the Sierra Nevada range and the Rocky Mountains. It receives between 18-30 cm (7-12 in) of rain each year. The Mojave Desert has at least 200 kinds of plants and animals that are not found in neighbouring deserts. It averages less than 15 cm (6 in) of rain each year.

The Sonoran Desert is the hottest desert in North America. However, some areas get rain twice a year, which allows a larger variety of plants and animals to thrive there. On average, this desert gets less than 38 cm (15 in) of rain each year.

DO THE MATHS!

Use the information in red in the Map-a-stat box to work out the following challenge. Make a bar graph showing the precipitation, or rainfall, in each desert every year. Which desert gets the least precipitation? You can use this chart to help you work out the answer, too.

Desert	Precipitation
Chihuahuan	25 cm or less
Great Basin	30 cm or less
Mojave	15 cm or less
Sonoran	38 cm or less

Complete the maths challenge, then turn to pages 28—29 to see if your calculation is correct!

Valley of Fire, Mojave Desert

Forests

The United States has 154 national forests, which are protected forest areas. Almost 50 per cent of Canada's land is covered by forests. Mexico also has a lot of forested land, including dry forests, pine and oak forests and the Lacandón Rainforest. Many of Mexico's forests cover its numerous mountain ranges.

Redwood forests

California and southwestern Oregon are home to the tallest tree species on Earth, the coast redwood. Redwood forests once covered 8,094 sq km (3,125 sq miles) of the Californian coast. However, logging has destroyed around 95 per cent of these forests. Today, national parks protect the remaining coast redwoods.

Black bears make their homes in forests across North America.

Giant sequoias are trees that can grow so large, it can take several people to reach around their trunks.

Hoh Forest

Map-a-stat

Hoh Forest, in Washington State, receives up to 432 cm (170 in) of rain each year. That is up to 4.27 m (14 ft.) of rain!

Canada's forests make up 10 per cent of the world's forests. Nearly 70 per cent of Canadian forests are coniferous, which means they are evergreen, cone-bearing trees.

Around 0.5 per cent of Mexico's forests are cut down each year. Much of this land is turned into pasture land for cattle.

Coast redwoods can grow to be 91 m (300 ft.) tall and many are 9 m (30 ft.) around. The oldest redwood lived for about 2,200 years, and there are many still living that are older than 600 years.

DO THE MATHS!

Use the information in red in the Map-a-stat box and the desert rainfall chart on page 21 to work out the following challenge. How much more rain does the Hoh Forest receive than all the North American deserts added together? Here is the equation to help you solve the problem.

$$432 \text{ cm} - (25 + 30 + 15 + 38)$$
$$= ? \text{ more cm of rain}$$

Complete the maths challenge, then turn to pages 28—29 to see if your calculation is correct!

Mountains

There are plenty of mountain ranges in North America with impressive peaks. Each of the three largest countries in North America has several peaks that are more than 4,572 m (15,000 ft.) tall. The three tallest peaks on the continent are Denali, or Mount McKinley, in Alaska, Mount Logan in Canada and Volcán Citlaltépetl in Mexico.

The Rocky Mountains

The Rocky Mountains, also called the Rockies, stretch from Canada to New Mexico. They were formed more than 35 million years ago. The highest peak in the Rockies is Mount Elbert in Colorado. It stands at 4,399 m (14,433 ft.) tall. The Rockies are home to bighorn sheep, moose, elk, deer, bears, coyotes and more. There are many forests in the range, as well.

Mount Logan

Denali

The Rocky Mountains

Volcán Citlaltépetl

The Aspen Highlands in Aspen, Colorado, are a top skiing destination.

Map-a-stat

Of the top 200 tallest mountains in North America, 159 are in the United States, 31 in Canada and there are 10 in Mexico. Many of the tallest US peaks are found in Alaska.

Alaska's Denali is 6,194 m (20,320 ft.) tall. Mount Logan, in Canada's Yukon Territory, is 5,959 m (19,551 ft.) tall and Volcán Citlaltápetl in Mexico is 5,610 m (18,406 ft.) tall.

North America's top three peaks do not even make the top 100 in the list of the world's highest peaks. The tallest mountain on Earth is Mount Everest at 8,850 m (29,035 ft.). The 100th tallest in the world is Mount Karjiang, in Tibet, which measures 7,221 m (23,691 ft.) tall.

The Rocky Mountains stretch 4,828 km (3,000 miles) from northern British Columbia in Canada all the way down to New Mexico.

Denali is the tallest peak in North America.

DO THE MATHS!

Bighorn sheep live in the Rocky Mountains.

Use the information in red in the Map-a-stat box to work out the following challenge. How much taller is Mount Everest than Denali? How much taller is the 100th tallest mountain in the world than Denali? Here are the equations to help you solve the problem.

$$8,850 \text{ m} - 6,194 \text{ m} = ? \text{ m}$$
$$7,221 \text{ m} - 6,194 \text{ m} = ? \text{ m}$$

Complete the maths challenge, then turn to pages 28–29 to see if your calculation is correct!

From sea to shining sea

North America is a beautiful continent. Its East Coast sits on the Atlantic Ocean and its West Coast borders the Pacific. In between, there are many different ecosystems, climates and geographic features. There are huge cities, tiny towns and vast wildernesses.

These colourful boats rest on an island beach off the coast of Mexico.

Banff National Park

Grand Canyon National Park

New York City

Mexico City

Much to explore

Amazing national parks, such as the Grand Canyon National Park in Arizona and the Banff National Park in Alberta, Canada, remind us what the continent might have been like before European settlers arrived. In contrast, beautiful, modern cities, such as Mexico City and New York City, remind us how far we have come. North America is certainly worth exploring!

Map-a-stat

Canada has many islands. Ellesmere Island is Canada's northernmost point. The island is the tenth-largest island in the world, yet, due to its climate, only 146 people live there.

Mexico City is the largest city in North America, with around 8.8 million people. New York City has the second-largest population, with 8.4 million people.

The Grand Canyon is more than 1,800 m (6,000 ft.) deep and 29 km (18 miles) wide.

Mexico has more than 30 UNESCO World Heritage Sites, which makes it a popular place to visit. UNESCO works to identify and keep safe important cultural, natural and historical places in the world.

Mission Santa Barbara

Northern Lights

DO THE MATHS!

Use the information in red in the Map-a-stat box to work out the following challenge. How many more people live in Mexico City than live in New York City? Here is the equation to help you solve the problem.

8,800,000 people – 8,400,000 people = ? people

Complete the maths challenge, then turn to pages 28—29 to see if your calculation is correct!

Maths challenge answers

You have made it through the mathalon!
How did your maths skills measure up?
Check your answers below.

Page 5

530,000,000 people –
(318,000,000 + 120,000,000 +
35,000,000) = 57,000,000 people

Page 7

25,000 polar bears – 15,000 polar bears
= 10,000 polar bears

Page 9

2,037 m – 105 m = 1,932 m taller

Page 11

2,782 km ÷ 3.2 km per hour = 869 hours

Page 13

(644 km ÷ 3.2 km per hour)
× 2 = 402 hours

Page 15

91 m – 1 m = 90 m

Page 17

201 km + 613 km = 814 km

Page 19

(91 steps ÷ 1 step per second) ÷ 60 seconds = 1.5 minutes

Page 21

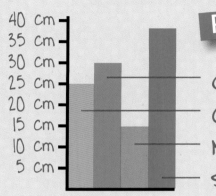

40 cm
35 cm
30 cm
25 cm
20 cm
15 cm
10 cm
5 cm

— Great Basin Desert
— Chihuahuan Desert
— Mojave Desert
— Sonoran Desert

The Mojave Desert gets the least precipitation.

Page 23

432 cm − (25 + 30 + 15 + 38) = 324 more cm of rain

Page 25

8,850 m − 6,194 m = 2,656 m

7,221 m − 6,194 m = 1,027 m

Page 27

8,800,000 people − 8,400,000 people
= 400,000 people

DO THE MATHS!

Glossary

adapted changed in order to survive

amphibian cold-blooded animal that spends part of its life in water and part on land

arid climate very hot, dry weather

barrier island island that is found near the coast and that forms a barrier between the coast and the ocean

bayou slow-moving body of water that flows out of lakes or rivers in the Southern United States

cactus plant with a tough, leathery stem or leaves that are covered with spines. They can survive in very dry places, such as deserts.

conquered overcame

constitution basic rules by which a country or a state is governed

continent one of Earth's seven large landmasses

cultural type of music, art, literature and customs of a people

ecosystem interconnected living things, such as animals and plants, and the non-living things, such as air and water, in one place

elevation height above sea level of an object or area

fertile describes ground that is rich and able to produce crops and other plants

geological relating to Earth's rocks and minerals

Greenland large, very cold island north west of Europe

mammal animal that has warm blood and often fur. Most mammals give birth to live young and feed their babies with milk from their bodies.

megadiverse having a high percentage of Earth's plant and animal species

mesa high landform with steep sides and flat tops

monarch king or queen

native people people who are born in a place and whose ancestors lived there

non-vascular not having a vascular system, which is a series of veins that transport fluid around the body

peninsula area of land that is surrounded on three sides by ocean

plain large, flat area of land often covered in grasses

prairie large, open area of grassland, especially in North America

preserve keep something from being lost or from going bad

reptile animal that has scales covering its body and that uses the sun to control its body temperature

sanctuary place where people or animals are kept safe

species single kind of living thing. All people are one species.

tectonic plate moving piece of Earth's crust, or the top layer of Earth

waterway stretch of water that is used to transport goods by boat or ship

wetland low-lying area, such as a marsh or swamp, where the ground is saturated with water

World Heritage Site place in the world that is protected for its beauty or importance

Find out more

Books

United States Atlas (National Geographic Kids),
(National Geographic Society, 2012)

USA (Countries in Our World), Lisa Klobuchar
(Franklin Watts, 2012)

USA: Everything You Ever Wanted to Know (Not For Parents),
(Lonely Planet, 2013)

USA (Horrible Histories), Terry Deary
(Scholastic, 2010)

Websites

Take a look at some maps of North America and colour them in at:
www.enchantedlearning.com/geography/namer

Find out about the monarch butterfly, one of Mexico's amazing
creatures, at:
www.learner.org/jnorth/search/MonarchNotes3.html#30

Discover more about North America at:
**travel.nationalgeographic.com/travel/continents/north-
america**

Read some fun facts about North America, at:
www.fun-facts.org.uk/america/north_america.htm

Index